Getting Through to the Man You Love

Also by Michele Weiner–Davis

Divorce Busting: A Step-by-Step Approach to Making
Your Marriage Loving Again

Change Your Life and Everyone in It

In Search of Solutions: A New Direction in Psychotherapy
(with William O'Hanlon)

Getting Through to the Man You Love

The No-Nonsense, No-Nagging Guide for Women

Michele Weiner-Davis

St. Martin's Griffin
New York

ISBN 1-58238-035-X

First published in the United States as *A Woman's Guide to Changing Her Man Without His Even Knowing It* by Golden Books Adult Publishing

10 9 8 7 6 5 4